CW01652450

M … e

About the series

Fast Track is a series of short, practical guides designed to get you up to speed on key business and management skills.

Written by experts with many years' experience in the field, each guide gives you instant access to key tips, advice and guidance – information you can put to work straightaway.

First six titles in the series

- Appraisal & Performance Management 1 85835 948 1
- Delegation 1 85835 953 8
- Leadership 1 85835 963 5
- Managing Attendance 1 85835 968 6
- Managing Conflict 1 85835 978 3
- Managing Time 1 85835 958 9

About the Series Editor

Andrew Forrest is Director of Learning and Development at The Industrial Society. He has over 30 years' experience working with and developing people.

Managing Attendance

Sue Morris

First published in 2001
The Industrial Society
Robert Hyde House
48 Bryanston Square
London W1H 2EA
Telephone: +44 (0)20 7479 2000

© The Industrial Society 2001

ISBN 1 85835 968 6

**British Library Cataloguing-in-Publication Data.
A catalogue record for this book is available from the British Library.**

All rights reserved. No part of this publication may be reproduced, stored in a retrieval system or transmitted, in any form or by any means, electronic, mechanical, photocopying, recording and/or otherwise without the prior written permission of the publishers. This book may not be lent, resold, hired out or otherwise disposed of by way of trade in any form, binding or cover other than that in which it is published without prior written consent of the publishers.

Advice in this book is intended as guidance only. Legislation is subject to change.

Sue Morris asserts her moral right to be identified as the author of this work.

Printed by: Cromwell Press
Cover image by: Digital Vision
Cover design by: Sign Design
The Industrial Society is a Registered Charity No. 290003

Contents

Introduction

People can be absent from work for a number of reasons – some of them very good reasons – but whatever the reason, absence is costly to organisations and needs to be managed effectively.

There are many different causes for non attendance at work, the most typical being:

- Sickness absence
- Unauthorised/casual non attendance
- Lateness
- Absence for personal/domestic reasons
- Absence for public duties, eg acting as a local councillor or trade union representative.

Designed for busy line managers, team leaders and supervisors, this book will help you identify the causes of absence and provide practical guidance on how to manage it. It also gives an overview of the implications of the **Disability Discrimination Act 1995** when dealing with sickness absences which may be associated with an employee's disability.

1

Managing attendance

This chapter considers:
> Why it is important to manage attendance effectively.

Good attendance at work is essential for business survival, and it is never too soon to think about how to encourage it. Before even making an offer of employment, good recruitment practice will include checking attendance records and employee references, the completion of health questionnaires or the provision of medical reports. Once your people are in place, an open, supportive culture will help keep them happy, motivated – and at work!

There are a number of reasons why people need to take time off work – the majority of which are genuine – and these absences need to be handled sensitively and fairly through carefully managed procedures. Of course, if reasons for absence don't appear genuine it can be demoralising for those who do attend work regularly if the absence is not tackled and others are seen to 'get away with it'.

You need to understand what kinds of absences are occurring in your workplace, and ensure that they are managed. Of course, your time is at a premium, but non attendance at work can be very costly and disruptive – it must be tackled.

Time will be well spent keeping accurate records and preparing some simple statistics to find out how big a problem non attendance is in your organisation, whether the problem is localised or within the organisation generally, and what the possible causes for non attendance are. By trying to identify and resolve the underlying causes of absence attendance will improve.

Summary checklist

- ✓ Non attendance at work is costly, disruptive and often demoralising.
- ✓ The time and money spent managing attendance will significantly reduce the overall costs of non attendance to your organisation.

2

The cost of absenteeism

This chapter explains:
> How to calculate the cost of the missing employee and identify whether there are particular trouble spots that need to be addressed.

The cost of absenteeism at work is substantial. For each day an employee is absent from work, it is costing a UK organisation around £500 or more. This cost includes not only sick pay for the absent employee, but also other overheads such as the cost of overtime working to provide cover for the absentee, administrative costs, lost production, etc.

Record keeping

Good record keeping is essential for the effective management of absenteeism. It will enable you to calculate the amount of time actually lost and classify the reasons for absence.

Absences such as holidays, maternity leave, jury service, etc are predictable and can be planned for; it is those other, less predictable, absences that need to be actively managed. In particular, sickness absence, lateness and other unplanned and unauthorised absences can cause significant disruption.

By keeping accurate records of absences, the reasons for them and their duration, you can identify which absences need a closer look and decide whether action needs to be taken. The following are examples of codes used on attendance record sheets to record different types of absence:

C Time off on a career break

D Time off for dependants' leave

H Approved paid holiday leave

L Approved leave without pay

M Maternity leave

P Parental leave

R Time off under statutory rights

S Uncertificated sickness absence

SC Sickness absence covered by a self-certificate

MC Sickness absence covered by a doctor's certificate

T Time off attending a training course

U Unauthorised absence.

Statistics

By analysing the cause of absences (eg illness, stress, accidents), patterns may emerge which may respond to positive action. For example, providing flu jabs may well be a worthwhile investment; a particular process or job may be exposed as being the root cause of ill health or accidents; a manager may have an unusual number of people off with stress: this could lead to an investigation into management style or pressure of work within the department. By looking carefully at the underlying causes you can identify what action needs to be taken to reduce these causes and, ultimately, the level of absenteeism. Appendix 2 gives some examples of underlying causes for absenteeism.

Remember, an analysis of the reasons for absence displayed in a pie chart or table can often have more impact than when it is presented in the form of raw statistics!

Looking at individual patterns of absence

If an individual's absences fall into a particular pattern, eg they are attached to holidays or weekends, or perhaps occur when a particularly unpopular task has to be done, then this can be discussed with the employee and an explanation sought! On a more sympathetic note, it may be that the anniversary of an unpleasant experience, such as the death of a close family member, may cause recurring emotional problems for which support may be possible. Or it may reveal an underlying medical condition which needs further exploration with the individual to try to identify what, if anything, can be done to help resolve it.

Absence level 'triggers'

Some employers have schemes whereby employees are interviewed formally about their absenteeism when they hit certain triggers, for example:

- After 10 days of continuous absence in the last 12 months, or
- After four spells of absence in the last 12 months.

Whilst this method provides consistency across the organisation in terms of when management initiate formal interviews to discuss attendance, the downside is that it also provides a level of absenteeism which employees can reach without fear of formal challenge. However, management should still hold return-to-work interviews and informal discussions if they are concerned about an employee's attendance record.

Summary checklist

- ✓ Good record keeping is essential.
- ✓ Analyse the underlying causes of absence.
- ✓ Look at ways of tackling the root cause – not just the problem.

3

Sickness absence

Sickness absence accounts for a large proportion of time lost in the workplace.

Ill health, serious injury or disability may result either in long-term sickness absence or frequent short-term spells of sickness absence over a prolonged period. Alternatively, an employee may have frequent short-term sickness absences which do not have any underlying medical condition but which relate to a number of different causes. The following chapters consider each of these scenarios separately.

4

Long-term sickness absence

This chapter offers advice on:
> How to deal with employees who have long-term chronic sickness problems resulting in weeks or months off work at a time.

Absence through long-term sickness needs to be handled carefully and sensitively, whilst taking into account the pressures on the business created by the absentee. It is also possible that the employee's illness or incapability may be regarded as a disability and therefore covered by the provisions of the **Disability Discrimination Act 1995**.

Clear rules

There should be clear rules for the employee to follow, indicating how they should keep in touch and how often; for example, weekly or monthly telephone calls to the line manager to advise on progress as well as the provision of medical certificates. Most organisations require a self-certification form to be completed after the first three days of absence and then a medical certificate from the employee's GP or other medical specialist to be submitted after seven days.

Not only should the employee be expected to keep in regular contact with their manager, but it is also good practice for the line manager to keep in touch with the employee. Some organisations will delegate this to a welfare or personnel officer depending upon the practicalities of the situation. This on-going contact serves a number of purposes:

- It helps prevent the employee feeling isolated from their workplace and smoothes their path back into work.
- It provides an opportunity for the employee to raise any worrying queries, eg sick pay concerns or outstanding work issues that may be playing on their mind.
- It keeps the employee up to date with news so that they continue to feel part of the team.
- It shows that the organisation cares.

What next?

There comes a time for most employers when they have to consider what to do next after an employee has been off sick for a prolonged period of time. What this period of time is depends very much on the size of an organisation and its resources, both in terms of financial and skills resources – ie its ability to cope while an employee is off sick.

It will also depend on whether the employee is likely to be able to return to some sort of work in the foreseeable future, and whether such work is available.

It will also depend on the cushion provided by any contractual benefit schemes offered to employees who become incapacitated through ill health (line managers would be advised to check with their Human Resources adviser on the implications of any contractual benefit schemes the organisation may provide).

A similar principle will apply to contractual sick pay in that a dismissal on the grounds of incapability prior to exhausting entitlement to contractual sickness benefit would be seen as depriving the employee of their contractual entitlement.

The organisation's sickness policy should also indicate that the employee may be requested to attend a medical appointment with a company-nominated doctor and/or to agree to a medical report being submitted by their own GP or medical adviser.

Many organisations retain the services of an occupational health physician to advise and support their decision making regarding prolonged sickness absence. This has the advantage of using your own medical expert to interpret the GP's or other medical adviser's reports/records in the light of the knowledge and experience they have gained of your working environment.

There are special rules to follow when obtaining a report from the employee's GP or a copy of their medical records and it is normally the HR department's function to manage this process.

Once the medical report or medical records have been received meet again with the employee to discuss the options available, eg:

- Lighter or alternative duties which are more suitable to the individual's capabilities.
- Shorter or different hours of work.
- Physical adjustments that could be made to work equipment or facilities.
- Permanent health insurance/invalidity benefit.
- Ill health retirement.

'Return-to-work' interviews

If the employee is able to return to work, in whatever capacity, then it is a good idea to conduct a 'return-to-work' interview before they return. An example return-to-work interview record is attached at

Appendix 1 providing examples of the sorts of questions that should be put to the employee together with a record of their responses.

The return-to-work interview serves a number of purposes:

- To establish whether any adjustments need to be made to the workplace or work equipment to enable the employee to function effectively.
- To establish whether some duties need to be phased back in if they are physically or mentally tiring to give the employee the chance to build up their stamina.
- To find out whether the employee is still on any medication which may affect their work, or whether any facilities need to be provided to take the medication. For example, if an employee with diabetes needs to inject insulin, is there a suitable room available for this purpose?
- It provides an opportunity to bring the employee up to date with developments/changes in working arrangements and discuss any re-training requirements.
- It shows that you are concerned for their welfare.

Depending on the nature of their work, some organisations will require the employee to attend their occupational health physician before the employee is allowed to resume work, even if the employee has been declared fit by their GP. In this way, professional medical advice can be taken on any limitations the employee may have on their return and advice given on any appropriate adjustments that need to be made.

Dismissal

An employer is not required to 'create' a special position for an employee who is unable to undertake their normal duties due to incapability, although suitable alternative work should be sought. If the employee suffers from a disability then any suitable adjustments should be made to the available job. If none of the above options is viable, and the employee's job can no longer be held open, then the employer may be left with no alternative but to consider dismissal on the grounds of the employee's incapability.

However, before this step is taken, the employee should be consulted and advised of the likelihood of dismissal. This will provide an opportunity to ensure that all avenues have been explored before employment is terminated. As with all meetings which could result in a decision to terminate employment, it would be wise to give the employee the opportunity of being accompanied so that they have some moral support. Similarly, the individual conducting this meeting on behalf of the organisation would be well advised to be accompanied.

If termination of employment becomes inevitable, then advice should be sought from your HR department to ensure that the employee receives their entitlements under their contract of employment.

What to do about conflicting medical advice

Occasionally, when seeking medical advice, there can be a difference of opinion between the advice given by the employee's GP and the organisation's occupational health physician. If this happens then you need to consider which is the most appropriate advice to take under the circumstances.

Normally it will be the employee's GP who is the better judge of the employee's health as he will have been involved in the clinical care of the individual, whereas the occupational health physician will be better placed to judge the effect of the employee's health in relation to the work and working environment.

At the end of the day it is up to management to decide on an employee's fitness for the work available, not a doctor, who is only in a position to provide the medical advice for making that decision.

Checklist

- ✓ Organisation rules for sickness absence should make it clear how and when the employee is expected to keep in touch.
- ✓ Periodic visits/phone calls should be made by the line manager or personnel manager to keep the employee in touch with the workplace, eg news of colleagues, news of developments in the department – but keep it low key and chatty.
- ✓ If prolonged absence means that continued employment could be at risk, discuss this with the employee and obtain medical advice from their GP or other medical adviser.
- ✓ Where further advice is needed about the employee's medical condition, consider arranging for the employee to be examined by an occupational health physician appointed by the organisation.
- ✓ When seeking written consent to obtain a medical report or a copy of the medical records, the employee must be advised of their rights.
- ✓ Once the medical report or medical records have been received meet again with the employee to discuss available options, eg return to work, what reasonable adjustments could be made, PHI/invalidity benefit schemes, ill health retirement.

- ✓ If the employee is able to return to work, carry out a return-to-work interview.
- ✓ If the decision is taken to dismiss, the employee should be given the notice to which they are entitled under their contract of employment and advised of any right of appeal.
- ✓ Allow the employee the opportunity of having a companion present at meetings and consider the need for a personal witness.
- ✓ Keep notes of all discussions and follow up key conversations in a letter to the employee.

Case study

In the well-estabished case of East Lindsay District Council v Daubney 1977 (IRLR) 181, Mr Daubney was employed as a surveyor and had been off sick following a mild stroke for around six months. He was covered by medical certificates which stated general debility.

The district community physician was asked to advise on whether Mr Daubney's state of health was such that he should be retired early on ill health grounds. The physician, who based his report on an examination carried out by another doctor from another area health authority, advised that he should be retired early and Daubney was subsequently sent a letter terminating his employment on the grounds of incapability.

Both the Industrial Tribunal and the Employment Appeals Tribunal found the dismissal unfair because East Lindsay District Council had dismissed Mr Daubney without obtaining a full medical report or giving him the opportunity to put his side of the story. They said that this may have brought to light new information of which his employers were unaware, or Mr Daubney might have wanted to seek medical advice on his own account which might have caused his employers to change their views.

Maternity-related sickness absence

If a female employee is off sick for a prolonged period of time it would be automatically unfair to dismiss her if the dismissal was because of a maternity-related illness. However, the employee should still be expected to keep in touch in accordance with your rules for sickness absence, and you with her. It may also be helpful to seek medical advice to find out if she is likely to be fit to return before the baby is born so that you can plan for cover, or to find out what sort of work she would be able to do and whether you need to make adjustments to accommodate her condition. If an employee is off sick for pregnancy-related reasons then her maternity leave is automatically triggered with effect from the sixth week before the expected week of childbirth. Following maternity leave, if the employee is unable to return to work for reasons unrelated to the pregnancy, then the normal organisation sickness rules will apply. If the sickness absence is related to the pregnancy then professional advice should be sought before considering what action to take.

Summary checklist

- ✓ Keep in regular contact with employees who are off sick for prolonged periods.
- ✓ Seek medical advice and discuss the options available to the employee before reaching any decision.
- ✓ If dismissal for incapability becomes inevitable, give notice if appropriate and the right to appeal.

5

Short-term sickness absence

This chapter offers advice on:

> How to deal with employees who have short spells of sickness absence including the odd day here or there, or even the odd couple of weeks here or there.

Short-term sickness absences are often more disruptive to manage than long-term sickness absences in that they are usually unpredictable and therefore difficult to provide cover for at short notice.

As with long-term sickness absences, organisation rules should make it clear what employees must do if they are unable to attend work through sickness absence. Ideally, they should be required to contact their line manager personally, either before they are due to start work or within the first hour of their normal start time, to advise of their sickness absence and likely return date.

It is the line manager or team leader who needs to know what is going on as soon as possible so that arrangements for cover can be made and any unfinished tasks identified. It will also be more uncomfortable for the employee who is not genuinely sick if they have to speak directly to their line manager or team leader rather than being able to leave a message, eg with reception, security or a friend!

When talking to an employee who has phoned in sick, maintain a balance between concern for their welfare and the need for them to be at work. Too much sympathy may lead them to believe they can take as much time as they like, when in fact they are fit enough to be at work. Too little sympathy and lack of support may result in the employee struggling to work when they are not well enough and could end up compounding the issue with complaints of stress and victimisation!

Return-to-work interviews should be carried out by the line manager for *all* sickness absences, even for absences of less than a day. Not only does this show genuine concern for the employee's well-being but it also enables the manager to explore the real reasons for the absence.

Often, when the time is taken to find out what is really behind an employee taking time off work, it becomes clear that the root cause of the absenteeism is something to do with matters which you may be able to influence. For example, there may be personality clashes within the team, there may be a training need which the employee is loathe to acknowledge but which causes anxiety and subsequently sickness absence.

See Appendix 2 for a fuller list of examples of underlying causes that could impact on attendance at work, and which you should try to identify and, where possible, work towards finding resolutions with the employee.

Obviously, the reasons given for sickness absence and the length of the sickness absence will impact on the content and approach of your return-to-work interview, but consider the following areas of discussion:

- Discuss sickness absence, even if it is for less than a day and the discussion is brief.
- Discuss sickness record even if it is covered by a medical certificate.
- Highlight any patterns of sickness absence.
- Try to identify any underlying causes of absence.
- Is there something which you could do to help resolve matters?
- Is the work itself affecting the employee's health?

- Does the employee's personal life impact on their ability to remain fit and healthy?
- Are there any underlying medical issues that need to be addressed?
- Are there any adjustments to the working environment or the job itself which could reasonably be made to help the employee?

If you are not satisfied that the absence was due to genuine sickness, then follow the guidelines on p. 28 for dealing with unauthorised/ casual non attendance.

Ideally, self-certification forms should be completed in the presence of the line manager and could be part of the return-to-work interview process.

If sickness absences persist, consider obtaining medical advice either through your occupational health adviser or through the employee's GP or medical adviser.

Advise the employee on the improvement needed in their attendance record, and that failure so to improve could lead to disciplinary action.

If attendance does not improve to an acceptable standard, instigate the disciplinary procedure, taking into account the employee's age, service, performance and the effect of their non attendance on the business.

Checklist

- ✓ Organisation rules should make it clear what employees must do if they are unable to attend work through sickness absence.
- ✓ Maintain a balance between concern for the employee's welfare and the need for them to be at work.
- ✓ Carry out return-to-work interviews for all absences.

- ✓ Explore with the employee possible underlying causes for the sickness absence.
- ✓ Consider whether there are any issues that need to be addressed or temporary adjustments that need to be made in working arrangements to support the employee.
- ✓ Consider obtaining medical advice.
- ✓ Advise on the improvement needed in the employee's attendance record and that the consequences of not achieving this could be disciplinary action.
- ✓ If attendance does not improve instigate the disciplinary procedure.

Case study

In International Sports Company v Thompson (1980) IRLR 340, Mrs Thompson was employed as a racket stringer. During the last 18 months of her employment she had been absent from work for some 25% of the time. At that time her employers had agreed with the trade union that 8% was an acceptable level.

The majority of Mrs Thompson's sickness absences were covered by medical certificates and were for a variety of different reasons, for example she suffered from conditions such as dizzy spells, anxiety and nerves, bronchitis, virus infection, cystitis, althruigra of the left knee, dyspepsia and flatulence.

Mrs Thompson received a series of warnings about her poor level of attendance, the last of which was a final written warning, but her level of attendance still remained high at 22% and she was subsequently dismissed for conduct.

The employers consulted their company doctor who took the view that no useful purpose would be served by seeing Mrs Thompson because he could see no common link between the illnesses, and as she was not suffering from any long-term chronic illness he was unable to give a view as to her future state of health.

The Industrial Tribunal found the decision unfair but the Employment Appeals Tribunal reversed this decision commenting that "It would be placing too heavy a burden on an employer to require him to carry out a formal medical investigation. Even if he did, such an investigation would rarely prove fruitful because of the transient nature of the employee's symptoms and complaints". The EAT was satisfied that the company had investigated her attendance record and had issued warnings and that in the light of Mrs Thompson's attendance record any employer was entitled to say 'enough was enough'.

However, in the case of Trico-Folberth Ltd v Devonshire (1989) IRLR 398, Mrs Devonshire had been given verbal and written warnings following a number of sickness-related absences. After a final spell of seven weeks' sickness absence with bronchitis she was dismissed for her unacceptable attendance record. Mrs Devonshire appealed against her dismissal and the panel changed the reasons for her dismissal, on compassionate grounds, from conduct to being medically unfit to do the job. The Tribunal held that dismissal for poor attendance would have been fair but because the employer had changed the reason for the dismissal to medical unfitness it was unfair because there had been insufficient investigation into her medical condition and insufficient consultation with her and her GP to justify dismissal on the grounds of ill health.

Maternity-related sickness absence

As with prolonged periods of sickness absence, if an employee is frequently off sick for short periods of time it would automatically be unfair to dismiss her if the dismissal was because of a maternity-related illness. However, it would still be appropriate to discuss any absences with her, and it may also be helpful to seek medical advice to find out whether you need to make adjustments to accommodate her condition and so facilitate her attendance at work.

Summary checklist

- ✓ Undertake return-to-work interviews to establish the cause of sickness absence.
- ✓ If appropriate seek medical advice.
- ✓ If absences persist, make the employee aware of any improvements needed and advise them that failure to improve could lead to disciplinary action and ultimately dismissal.
- ✓ Be clear about whether you are dismissing on grounds of poor attendance or incapability.

6

Implications of the Disability Discrimination Act 1995

This chapter offers advice on:
> How to deal with sickness absence when an employee has a disability as defined by the **Disability Discrimination Act 1995**.

The **Disability Discrimination Act 1995** makes it unlawful to discriminate against an individual on account of a disability. When dealing with absenteeism, discrimination occurs when a disabled person is treated less favourably for a reason related to their disability, or where the employer fails to make reasonable adjustments to employment arrangements where the individual is placed at a substantial disadvantage, unless there is justification for doing so.

There may be some sickness absences, which may be long-term sickness absences or short-term persistent sickness absences, involving employees with disabilities. If those absences which relate to the disability are taken into account then the employer will have to show that it was justified in doing so in all the circumstances, for example the size and resources of the organisation will affect how it can cope with these absences; how key the employee's ability to attend work regularly is to the business.

Case study

In the case of Cox v Post Office, Mr Cox was a postman who was dismissed following excessive absenteeism due to asthma. The Tribunal considered that the importance of maintaining an efficient service and ensuring letters were delivered on time (and that staff therefore needed to attend work regularly to perform those duties) had relevance. However, the Tribunal found no evidence that Mr Cox's absences had caused any cost to the Post Office or any disruption to the business, or that it was an unreasonable burden to cover for his absences such as to justify his dismissal. The Tribunal considered that a reasonable adjustment to their attendance procedure would have been for the employer to review Mr Cox's attendance record, having excluded absences that were related to his disability. In this case the Tribunal held that the employer had failed to make reasonable adjustments to accommodate his disability and that there was no justification for not so doing.

A disability is defined by the Act as a "physical or mental impairment which has a substantial and long-term adverse affect on a person's ability to carry out normal day-to-day activities". An "impairment" is "long-term" if it has lasted, or is likely to last, at least 12 months, whether continuous or intermittent, and have a substantial adverse affect on the individual's ability to undertake one or more of the following normal day-to-day activities:

- Mobility, eg difficulty with travelling or walking.
- Manual dexterity, eg loss or limited use in one or both hands.
- Physical co-ordination, eg difficulty in pouring liquid into a cup.
- Continence, eg infrequent loss of control such as once a month.

- Ability to lift, carry or move everyday objects, eg unable to pick up light objects.
- Speech, eg unable to communicate clearly.
- Hearing, eg difficulty in holding a conversation in a moderately noisy environment.
- Eyesight, eg unable to pass the eyesight test for a standard driving test or distinguish colours.
- Memory or ability to concentrate, learn or understand, eg persistent inability to remember the names of familiar people or write a cheque without help.
- Perception of the risk of physical danger, eg unable to tell by touch that an object is very hot or cold.

Normal day-to-day activities also include domestic activities, shopping and leisure activities.

If an employee is placed at a substantial disadvantage in undertaking their normal day-to-day activities because of a disability, the organisation has a duty to make reasonable adjustments wherever possible to accommodate that person's disability.

The Act gives examples of what adjustments an employer may have to make, including:

- Making reasonable physical or structural adjustments to premises, eg widening doorways, providing ramps, moving light switches, door handles, shelves, improving lighting.
- Allocating some of the disabled person's duties to another person, eg if the job involves occasional lifting of objects then this aspect of the job may have to be done by somebody else if an employee suffers a disability affecting their ability to lift.
- Transferring the person to fill an existing vacancy, eg suitable alternative available work should be sought and, where appropriate, reasonable training provided.

- Altering the person's working hours, eg allowing more flexibility in working arrangements.
- Changing the place of work, eg transferring the employee to more accessible premises or to a different floor in the building.
- Allowing the person to be absent more often during working hours than a person without a disability for rehabilitation, assessment or treatment, eg more time off than would normally be granted for a non disabled person.
- Training, eg training in the use of equipment specific to the disability, or adapting training methods to suit the abilities of a disabled person.
- Acquiring or modifying equipment, eg specially adapted keyboards or telephones.
- Modifying instructions or reference manuals, eg produced on braille or cassette, or individual oral training for people with learning disabilities.
- Modifying procedures for testing or assessment, eg to accommodate a person with dyslexia or restricted hand/arm movement.
- Providing a reader or sign language interpreter, eg to read mail or other correspondence.
- Providing supervision, eg a mentor or support worker where disability leads to uncertainty or lack of confidence.

Many adjustments can be made with little or no cost or disruption to the organisation. However, when deciding what is a reasonable adjustment to make the Act lists a number of issues that need to be considered, eg:

- The effectiveness of the adjustment in preventing disadvantage to the disabled person.

- Whether it is practicable for the employer to make the adjustment.
- The financial costs and the extent of any disruption caused.
- The employer's financial and other resources.
- The availability of financial or other assistance towards making the adjustment.

Summary checklist

✓ If an employee is unable to attend work on a regular basis as a result of a disability seek professional advice.

✓ Consult with the employee on the options available.

✓ Look at what reasonable adjustments can be made to both the premises, the location of the job and the job itself.

7

Unauthorised/casual non attendance

> This chapter considers:
> > How to deal with employees who don't turn up for work – malingerers.

Although it probably only involves a minority of employees, employees who do not turn up for work without good reason cause not only frustration to their colleagues but also disruption to the organisation's business.

If there has been no contact or explanation provided by the employee for their absence, try to get in touch. Ask their work mates if they know of any reason why the employee has not turned up for work; try telephoning the contact numbers provided by the missing employee; if it is practicable, call round to the last known address armed with a letter seeking an explanation for the absence (in case there is no-one at home note on the envelope that the letter should be forwarded if appropriate). Don't be tempted to prejudge the reasons for the absence until you have established the facts: the missing employee may be malingering or enjoying other activities that are more attractive than attending work; alternatively, there may be a genuine problem which may need your understanding and support.

As with any absence from work, return-to-work interviews should be carried out by the line manager immediately on the employee's return to establish the reason for the non attendance and, if appropriate, why the employee failed to get in touch.

Explore with the employee the reasons for their non-attendance before deciding what action to take: it could be a genuine health problem; it could be a genuine domestic or personal problem. If it is, then refer to Appendix 2.

If the employee is unable to give a satisfactory explanation for their non attendance, then instigate the disciplinary procedure.

It is essential that unauthorised absence is dealt with firmly and consistently so that employees understand they cannot simply not turn up for work when they have better things to do and think they can get away with it. Also, those who do attend work regularly and punctually will appreciate not having to carry 'passengers' and will apply peer pressure to their colleagues not to let the side down.

Checklist

- ✓ Carry out return-to-work interviews.
- ✓ Explore the reasons for non attendance.
- ✓ Identify any underlying causes.
- ✓ If there is no satisfactory explanation, instigate the disciplinary procedure.

Case study

In Hutchinson v Enfield Rolling Mills Ltd (1981) IRLR 318 EAT, Mr Hutchinson had been given a medical certificate on Monday 30

April for seven days stating he was suffering from sciatica. On 1 May he was seen by a company director taking part in a union demonstration in Brighton, far away from his place of work. He was subsequently dismissed on the grounds that his presence in Brighton "was not consistent with a person who was reputedly suffering from sciatica. In other words, if you were fit enough to travel to Brighton to take part in a demonstration, you were fit enough to report for work".

An Industrial Tribunal concluded that that it was none of the employer's business what the employee chose to do during his certified sick leave, but the EAT overturned this stating that a medical certificate does not give an employee the freedom to do whatever he likes. It was established that an employer is entitled to 'go behind' a doctor's sick note to investigate the true reasons for an employee's absence from work and, if appropriate, to challenge the certificate.

Checklist

✓ Review the attendance record with the employee and give them the opportunity to put forward their side of the story.

✓ Always try to find the underlying causes for absences – there may be issues affecting the employee's ability to attend work regularly for which you can give support and guidance.

✓ If attendance does not improve, instigate the disciplinary procedure.

How to deal with the disappearing employee

Sometimes employees simply disappear and you don't know if it is their intention to return to work or not, or whether they have simply decided to leave and take up employment elsewhere.

If this occurs, then the employer must make enquiries before jumping to conclusions. There is always the possibility that something may have befallen the employee, for example a close relative may have had been taken seriously ill or have died and the employee may have had to go away suddenly to deal with matters; the employee themselves may have been injured in a serious accident and not be in a position to get in touch!

Try contacting the employee by telephone or, if practicable, by personal visit, or by letter to their last known address and ask for an explanation.

If you receive no response to your telephone messages, or there is nobody at home or no response to your letter, write to the employee again, this time sending it by recorded delivery. Express your concerns about their non attendance and lack of communication. Ask for an explanation of their absence and advise them that unless you hear from them within a reasonable period of time, eg 10 calendar days, you will have no alternative but to infer that they have repudiated their contract and you will be treating their employment as terminated.

If you receive no response to this letter, write again to the employee confirming that having received no response to your earlier communications, you are now dismissing them and enclose any outstanding pay due together with the P45.

If you are subsequently contacted by the ex-employee to question your actions within a reasonable period of time, arrange to meet with the individual so they can put forward an explanation for their behaviour.

Having heard the explanation you may (or may not, depending on the circumstances) wish to review your decision.

In treating the absence as a repudiation of the employee's contract of employment, you then need to consider whether the employee has any rights against the organisation. For example, the employee may have sufficient service to make a claim of unfair dismissal. However, failing to attend work indefinitely without a reasonable explanation would be viewed as an act of gross misconduct which would normally result in dismissal without notice or payment in lieu of notice, although all other payments due under the contract of employment would continue to be due, eg outstanding holiday pay.

You could sue the employee for breach of contract and make a claim for losses sustained as a result of their repudiation, although most employers don't bother as the time and cost of doing so is not usually worth the effort.

Checklist

- ✓ Don't jump to conclusions – try to get in touch!
- ✓ If you receive no response, write to the employee giving them a timescale in which to respond.
- ✓ If yet again you receive no response, write again advising that you are now treating their employment as terminated.
- ✓ If you are subsequently contacted, arrange to meet the employee and listen to their explanation.
- ✓ Review your decision.

8

Holidays

This chapter offers advice on:
> How to resolve problems concerned with holidays.

Under the Working Time Directive employees are now entitled to a minimum of four weeks' statutory holiday per annum. This minimum entitlement includes the eight statutory bank holidays. Under the statutory scheme, employees are required to give at least twice the number of days notice as the amount of holiday which they wish to take, although alternative arrangements can be agreed. For example, if an employee wishes to take a fortnight's leave then they must give you four weeks notice. If you are unable to agree to the holiday dates requested for business reasons, then the employer must give at least the same number of days notice as the holiday to postpone it.

From time to time employees who have been refused the amount of leave they desire take matters into their own hands by not returning to work on the due date.

Late return from normal holidays

If an employee fails to return to work on the due date after taking holiday then they may be in breach of contract. However, whether or not it is sufficiently serious to warrant disciplinary action or dismissal will depend on the seriousness of the breach and the reasons for the failure to return to work. For example, if the employee has behaved in a similar way on previous occasions and has received disciplinary warnings for this behaviour, or if he/she has been refused additional days of leave and has been warned that taking the additional days would result in dismissal, then dismissal is likely to be seen as fair.

However, as with all disciplinary matters, a fair procedure should be followed including proper investigation into the reasons for the failure to return to work before any action is taken.

Case study

In London Transport Executive v Clark (1981 IRLR 166), Mr Clark, who was born in Jamaica, was employed as a bus mechanic. London Transport had a rule which limited unpaid leave for overseas visits being taken not more frequently than every three years.

Mr Clark put in a request to take six weeks' unpaid leave to take a holiday in Jamaica. His application was refused because of his unsatisfactory work and sickness record and also because he had already taken unpaid leave within the last three years. Mr Clark asked what would happen if he went without permission and was told that there was an established procedure which would lead to him being removed from the books.

Mr Clark went on his holiday and London Transport wrote to his London address requesting an explanation for his absence. A week later he was written to again and given 14 days in which to respond or it would be assumed he did not wish to continue his employment. They subsequently wrote informing Mr Clark that his name had been permanently removed from their books.

Mr Clark claimed that he had been unfairly dismissed and the Court of Appeal held that both the Industrial Tribunal and the Employment Appeal Tribunal had correctly concluded that Mr Clark had not "self dismissed" but that his employment was terminated following London Transport's acceptance of his conduct as a repudiation of the contract.

In another case, Igbo v Johnson Matthey Chemicals Ltd (1986) IRLR 215 CA, Mrs Igbo had been granted extended leave to visit her family in Nigeria on condition that she signed a "contractual letter for the provision of extended holiday absence". It also included a statement which said "you are required to work your normal shift... immediately after the end of your holiday. This has been explained to you and you have agreed to return to work on (date). If you fail to do this your contract of employment will automatically terminate on that date."

Mrs Igbo returned to England but felt unwell and did not attend work on the due date but sent in a medical certificate to cover her absence. Her employer subsequently terminated her employment on the basis that she had failed to return to work as stated in the holiday agreement.

Mrs Igbo's claim that she had been unfairly dismissed was upheld by the Court of Appeal because the law does not allow an employee (other than a few exceptions) to contract out of their statutory right not to be unfairly dismissed and therefore the holiday agreement which provided for the termination of her employment if she did not return on the due date was void.

Late return from extended holidays

Many employers are willing to allow employees to take extended holidays, either by taking the extra days unpaid or by accruing some of their annual leave entitlement from adjoining holiday years. However, bear in mind that the Working Time Regulations require an employee to have the opportunity of taking a minimum of four weeks' paid holiday in a full holiday year, subject to them having acquired sufficient service to qualify.

It is not unusual for organisations with such a scheme to require an employee, prior to going on holiday, to sign a written agreement which confirms the dates of the holiday and that a failure to return to work on the due date will result in dismissal for gross misconduct. It should be noted that an agreement automatically to terminate employment if an employee fails to turn up for work on the expected date is void.

However, if an employer investigates and subsequently concludes that there has been an act of gross misconduct, then dismissal for gross misconduct may well be upheld as fair.

Case study

In Ali v Joseph Dawson Limited EAT 43/89, the company had employed a large number of people who came from Pakistan or India and who, from time to time, wanted to take extended leave to return to their homeland or make a pilgrimage to Mecca. Due to the numbers of employees wishing to take extended leave the company introduced a scheme which was intended to benefit both the employees and the company, but which made it quite clear that failure to comply with the terms of the scheme would likely result in dismissal.

Mr Ali asked for extended leave to visit Mecca and was asked to sign a letter agreeing to work up to a specified date and to be back at work on or before a specified date. He was notified that failure to meet this deadline would mean dismissal without notice or payment in lieu of notice.

Unfortunately, Mr Ali was delayed on his return because he left for his holiday without the appropriate paperwork enabling him to return to the UK, and on his return to work, following a five-minute investigation, he was dismissed. Mr Ali took his complaint to an Industrial Tribunal who held that his dismissal was fair, particularly given that he had been made aware of the likely consequences of a failure to return by the specified date.

Summary checklist

- ✓ Even when an employee has apparently 'disappeared' and there is no indication of any attempt by the individual to explain their absence, it is essential to make enquiries before jumping to the conclusion that they have left.

- ✓ If the employee does not respond to requests to get in touch, then it is safe to terminate employment.

- ✓ Failing to attend for work on an indefinite basis without offering a reasonable explanation would be viewed as an act of gross misconduct.

9

Lateness

This chapter considers:
> What to do about individuals who are unable to attend work on time.

Some organisations operate either an informal or formal flex-time approach to time-keeping which means that lateness is not an issue.

However, there are other organisations where punctuality is crucial to the business and the service they provide, in which case organisation rules regarding time-keeping and the importance of punctuality should be made known at recruitment.

There are many reasons why people have difficulty attending work on time and you need to adapt your approach to meet the different circumstances.

There is always going to be the rare occasion when the best time-keeper is late and it would clearly be unfair and unwise to make a big issue of it. However, if lateness is starting to give cause for concern then as a first step you should interview employees informally to advise them of your concerns about their attendance and to seek an explanation for their lateness.

Accurate records should be kept of employees' lateness together with any explanations for this.

When seeking an explanation for lateness, try to establish whether there are any underlying causes which might be affecting the individual's ability to attend on time in the short term. For example, are there personal problems such as illness in the family or illness of the child minder which makes it difficult for the employee to be punctual? These difficulties may be resolved by the employee's ability to take dependants' leave or parental leave.

If the employee does have temporary domestic problems, try to reach a short-term compromise by giving them time and space to resolve these issues without incurring further wrath from yourself! For example, short-term alternative working arrangements, use of unpaid leave, parental leave or annual leave, undertaking some work at home.

Don't leave matters open-ended – set a deadline at which you will review the position so the employee understands the need to make appropriate arrangements to resolve their difficulties.

If the issue is long term and insurmountable, consider alternative solutions with the employee, eg alternative working arrangements, use of unpaid or annual leave, working from home for some of the time.

If the employee has no plausible explanation for their lateness then use the disciplinary procedure.

Checklist

- ✓ Make organisation rules regarding time-keeping and the importance of punctuality known to employees.
- ✓ As a first step, interview employees informally to advise them of your concerns about their attendance record and to seek an explanation for their lateness.
- ✓ Keep accurate records of employees' lateness together with their explanations.
- ✓ Establish whether there are any underlying causes.

- ✓ If the employee does have temporary domestic problems, try to reach a short-term compromise.
- ✓ Don't leave matters open-ended – set a deadline at which you will review the position.
- ✓ If the issue is long term and insurmountable, consider alternative solutions.
- ✓ If the employee does not have a plausible explanation then use the disciplinary procedure.

Case study

John worked as a technical salesman for an office equipment manufacturer. His duties included manning a technical helpline one day a week on a rota basis with his colleagues and also setting up and promoting the company's products at exhibitions and at client sites by invitation, as well as his other sales responsibilities.

Unfortunately, John's time-keeping had become progressively worse – he was often up to half an hour late arriving for work and customers phoning the helpline had started to complain that there was no one there to take their calls. He had also arrived late on a number of client visits and at the last exhibition had been conspicuous by his absence until mid-morning.

When interviewed by his line manager, John was given the chance to raise any issues which were affecting his ability to attend work on time, but his only explanation was that there were roadworks close to where he lived and it was taking him longer to reach his destination.

John's manager reminded him of the need for punctuality in his role and tried to impress on him that he should allow for these sorts of contingencies. Unfortunately, John was not willing to make allowances to overcome delays to his journeys, nor did he come up with any explanation why he could not do so, only that he couldn't see why he should. Matters did not improve and there followed a series of disciplinary warnings for misconduct. John was eventually dismissed.

Summary checklist

- ✓ Make sure that employees are aware if they are in time critical posts.
- ✓ Raise any concerns about time-keeping promptly.
- ✓ Explore reasons for lateness.
- ✓ Where genuine short-term difficulties occur reach temporary arrangements with the employee, allow them 'space' to help resolve these issues.
- ✓ Agree timescales for improvement.
- ✓ If longer term, try to agree alternative working arrangements to suit both parties.
- ✓ If lateness persists follow the disciplinary procedure.

10

Absences for personal/domestic reasons

This chapter advises on:
> How to deal with absences for time off to deal with a variety of different emergencies or other personal/domestic matters.

1 Time off for dependants

All employees are entitled to reasonable unpaid time off work to deal with an emergency involving a dependant and to make any necessary longer-term arrangements.

Examples of unexpected or sudden problems

- If a dependant falls ill, has been involved in an accident or been assaulted (including where the victim is hurt or distressed rather than injured physically).
- When a partner is having a baby.
- To make longer-term care arrangements for a dependant who is ill or injured.
- To deal with the death of a dependant; for example, to make funeral arrangements or to attend a funeral.

- To deal with an unexpected disruption or breakdown in care arrangements for a dependant; for example, when a child minder or nurse fails to turn up.
- To deal with an incident involving the employee's child during school hours; for example, if the child has been involved in a fight or is being suspended from school.

Dependants

A dependant is the partner, child or parent of the employee or someone who lives with the employee as part of their family, for example, an elderly aunt or grandparent who lives in the household.

It does not include people such as tenants, boarders or resident household staff.

Time limits

There is no set limit to the amount of time off which can be taken, though it will normally be one or two days at the most. For example, if a child falls ill the leave should be enough to help the employee cope with the crisis, eg the immediate care of the child, visiting the doctor and making longer-term care arrangements, but not for the ongoing care of the child. Alternative arrangements such as the use of parental leave can be taken for this purpose.

Notice to employers

So that leave can be managed, procedures should be drawn up making it clear that employees should advise their employers as soon as possible about their absence, the reason for it and how long they expect to be away.

Although under the statutory scheme there is no requirement to keep records, it is recommended that a record of all such absences is kept, detailing the reasons for, and the period of, the absences so that they can be monitored. As with other absences, there should be return-to-work interviews and employees should be required to complete self-certification absence forms to cover these absences.

2 Compassionate leave

There is no statutory requirement to grant compassionate leave, although it is highly likely that if an employer dismissed an employee for taking such absence after it was requested and subsequently refused the employer would be seen to be acting unfairly. However, dependants' leave and parental leave will cover a number of these situations.

Many employers grant leave on compassionate grounds for certain situations such as bereavements and the funerals of close family members, marriage, looking after sick children or close family members. This may overlap with dependants' leave described above. It may be helpful to have written guidelines on how much time off is normally granted under the different circumstances, and whether or not it is paid or unpaid, or whether payment is solely at the discretion of the organisation.

As with dependants' leave, procedures should be drawn up to guide managers on how to manage requests for such leave, whether it must be taken as paid or unpaid leave, and to advise employees on how to go about making a request for time off in these circumstances. As above, requests for such absences and the arrangements agreed should be monitored.

3 Domestic/personal leave

There will be occasions when employees need to take time off to deal with domestic issues which are not strictly emergencies, but which nonetheless require time off to manage, eg getting married, moving house, arranging for services such as cookers, central heating systems to be repaired, to attend doctors, hospital or dental appointments.

Most organisations will allow employees to take one or two days' authorised leave with pay when they are getting married or moving house as a gesture of goodwill. Other appointments may well be treated in a variety of different ways. For example, employers who operate flexitime may well expect employees to organise these appointments in their own time, others may require employees to take it out of their annual leave or as authorised unpaid leave. Some organisations designate a small number of paid days per year which employees may use to attend to such matters; others will operate on a give and take basis, allowing time off with pay during the working day on the general understanding that employees will not 'clock watch' when jobs need to be finished at the end of the normal working day.

Whatever your arrangements, employees need to know what rules and procedures they are expected to follow, eg who they should approach to request time off, whether they will be paid or will have to make the time up.

Summary checklist

✓ Establish clear policies and procedures for dealing with emergency leave and requests for domestic/personal leave.

11

Imprisonment

This chapter offers advice on:
> How to manage the situation when you are advised that one of your employees has been remanded in custody or is in prison.

An employee who is in prison or remanded in custody is unavailable for work and is therefore not entitled to be paid remuneration. However, the fact that an employee is unable to attend work because they are incarcerated does not mean that employment can automatically be terminated.

In considering whether termination of employment is an appropriate action there are a number of factors that need to be taken into account, eg:

- Whether the offence is work related.
- Where the offence is not work related but impacts on the employee's ability to do their job, eg through their integrity or credibility being damaged.
- The employee's past performance and length of service.
- The period of time the employee is expected to be unavailable for work.
- Whether the employee is on remand or has been convicted.
- The disruption that will be caused by the employee's absence.

Where the offence is work related or impacts on the employee's ability to do their job, the normal disciplinary procedure should be followed. As a fair procedure involves allowing the employee the chance to put their side of the story before a decision is taken, you will have to look at alternative ways of providing this opportunity, for example, by the employee submitting written representations or by communicating via their solicitor.

It may be that after a certain period of absence it could be argued that the contract has been frustrated, in which case there is no requirement for notice to be given by either party as there is no "dismissal" on termination . Since it can be difficult to decide when a contract can be viewed as being "frustrated" it is usually safer to dismiss by following a fair procedure.

Case study

In Shepherd FC & Co Ltd V Jerrom (1986) IRLR 358 CA, Mr Jerrom, an apprentice plumber, was convicted of offences relating to his involvement in a motor cycle gang fight and sentenced to Borstal for between six months and two years. The Court of Appeal held that the contract had been frustrated.

Summary checklist

- ✓ Follow a fair procedure before taking the decision to dismiss.
- ✓ Consider the employee's past history and service.

- ✓ Consider the period of absence and the needs of the business.
- ✓ Consider what impact the offence has on the employee's ability to do the job.
- ✓ Provide an opportunity for the employee to state their case before reaching a decision.

12

Public duties

This chapter considers:
> How to deal with requests for time off work from employees who undertake public duties.

An employee is entitled to reasonable time off work to perform certain public duties which they have volunteered to do. These duties include:

- Justice of the Peace
- Member of a local authority
- Member of any statutory tribunal
- Member of a relevant heath body
- Member of a board of prison visitors, or a prison visiting committee
- Member of a police authority
- Member of a relevant education body
- Member of the Environment Agency or the Scottish Environment Protection Agency
- Member of a Service Authority for the National Criminal Intelligence Service or the Service Authority for the National Crime Squad.

There is no requirement to pay employees who take time off to undertake these duties, although many employers will negotiate with their employees to make payment for an agreed number of days.

Public duties include attending meetings of the relevant body, or undertaking any other activity approved by the relevant body or that is necessary for the body to function effectively, eg visits to schools, prisons, attending *ad hoc* meetings to deal with urgent issues and training.

In determining what is "reasonable" time off, the following circumstances may be taken into account:

- The impact of the time off on the employer's business.
- The amount of time spent by the employee taking time off for trade union duties or activities.
- How much time off is required for the performance of the public duties, and how much time off is required for the performance of that particular duty.

A degree of flexibility is expected both from employers and employees to accommodate an employee's participation in public duties. Ideally, you should discuss with prospective employees prior to offering employment, or with existing employees prior to their agreeing to take on public duties, what their needs for time off are likely to be so that arrangements can be agreed beforehand, eg the amount of anticipated time off, when it is likely to be needed, how pay will be affected, whether cover needs to be arranged.

Case study

In RJ Emmerson v Commissioners of Inland Revenue (1977) IRLR 458 IT, Mr Emmerson was employed as a training officer and became leader of the opposition of Portsmouth City Council. He had already been granted 18 days' paid leave and it had been assessed that in view of his position on the Council a reasonable amount of time off would be 30 days. The Tribunal acknowledged that the additional days would have some adverse affect on his work but that the employers should be able to allow him around a further 12 days without pay and, if necessary, they could appoint a deputy to cover his training duties. They also stated that Mr Emmerson should be prepared to use some of his annual leave to cover any additional days beyond the 30 days.

Summary checklist

- ✓ Where possible, discuss with prospective employees what their needs are for time off to undertake public duties so that you can consider the implications on the business and arrangements can be agreed in principle.
- ✓ Encourage existing employees to discuss with you their plans to take on public duties before they have committed themselves so that, as above, implications can be discussed and arrangements agreed.

13

Jury service

This chapter advises on:
> What to do if an employee is requested to attend jury service.

From time to time you will be advised by an employee that they have been summonsed to do jury service and you will be required to release them. It is possible for the employee to write to the Jury Summoning Officer asking to be excused if there is a good reason for doing so. For example, if the employer has genuinely good business reasons why the employee cannot be spared and provides the employee with a letter which they can then forward to the Jury Summoning Officer explaining this, then jury service may be postponed.

There is no statutory requirement for the employer to continue to pay the employee while attending jury service, although most do so. There are set amounts which an employee can claim from the courts for financial loss, subsistence and travel. If you decide to maintain your employee's pay while they attend jury service then it is wise to reach agreement with them to refund to the organisation the compensation they receive from the courts for financial loss or agree to make a deduction in their pay to compensate for it.

Consider including a section in your employee handbook or staff manual requesting employees to make you aware as soon as they have received a summons for jury service so their absence can be planned for well in advance. Arrangements for pay can then be agreed as suggested above.

Summary checklist

- ✓ Advise employees to notify you of any summons as soon as possible.
- ✓ If pay is to be continued during jury service make arrangements to offset the financial loss allowance against normal pay.

14

Statutory time off work

> This chapter considers:
> > How to deal with requests from trade union representatives or elected representatives for time off work to deal with their union/ representative duties.

There are a number of circumstances, apart from the undertaking of public duties, where employees are entitled to take time off work, either with or without pay.

Trade union shop stewards/representatives

An employee who has been elected as a shop steward/representative of a recognised independent trade union is entitled to take reasonable paid time off during working hours to undertake specified trade union duties, to undergo relevant training or to act as a companion at discipline and grievance hearings.

Specified union duties include:

- Duties concerned with negotiations in connection with collective bargaining for which the trade union is recognised.
- Duties performed on behalf of work colleagues where such duties have been agreed between the employer and union.

- Receiving information and consultation meetings in connection with redundancy or transfer of undertakings.

Relevant training includes:

- Training in relation to the above duties where approved by the TUC or the independent trade union.

The amount of time off and the frequency must be reasonable both in relation to balancing the needs of the trade union member and the employer. ACAS has produced a Code of Practice for Time Off for Trade Union Duties which gives guidelines and recommends that employers and trade unions reach agreement on the arrangements for time off.

The Code of Practice also includes issues to take into account when making arrangements for time off, eg:

- Communicating with shift workers and part-timers.
- Security and health and safety arrangements.
- Implications for work processes.

Time off for union activities

Members of independent recognised trade unions are entitled to reasonable unpaid time off during working hours to participate in appropriate union activities.

Appropriate union activities include:

- Attending normal union meetings.
- Voting in union elections and ballots.

The Code of Practice referred to above recommends that specific agreement is reached between employers and trade unions on issues such as when time off will be granted, procedures for requesting time off, if and when it will be paid.

Elected representatives

An employee who has been elected to act as an employee representative for consultation purposes regarding potential redundancies or transfers of undertakings is entitled to reasonable paid time off during working hours to undertake their duties or to undertake training relating to these duties. The amount of paid time off is as previously described for trade union officials.

Safety representatives

A recognised independent trade union may appoint safety representatives under the **Health and Safety at Work etc Act 1974 (HASAWA).** They are entitled to paid time off during working hours to undertake their "statutory" functions and reasonable time off for training.

The statutory functions include:

- Keeping safety arrangements under continual review.
- Investigating potential hazards.
- Making representations to the employer on specific and general health and safety matters.
- Making periodic examinations of the workplace at least once every three months.

The Health and Safety Commission has issued a Code of Practice which recommends that safety representatives receive basic training in performing their functions on appointment, including a grounding in general health and safety law, the nature and extent of hazards at work, the employer's policies and administrative arrangements concerning health and safety, and the appropriate skills needed properly to use the information obtained from their employer and from their periodic examinations.

Where there is no recognised independent trade union, representatives of employee safety may be elected. Their functions include:

- Making representations to the employer of potential hazards and dangerous occurrences in the workplace.
- Making general representations to the employer on general matters affecting health and safety.
- Representing their group of employees in consultations at the workplace with inspectors appointed under the HASAWA.

Summary checklist

✓ Reach agreement with recognised trade unions or elected representatives on the issues in which they will be involved.

✓ Reach agreement on the procedures for requesting time off work to undertake their duties or attend training.

✓ Reach agreement on the amount of time off that is likely to be needed.

Appendix 1

Example return-to-work interview record

Questions to employee

1 Are you fully recovered? YES/NO
If not, please give brief details

2 Are you fit to carry out your full range of duties? YES/NO
If not, please give details

3 Are you taking any medication that may affect your ability to carry out your duties? YES/NO
If yes, please give details

4 Do you require any further advice or support? YES/NO
If yes, please give details

5 Do you require any further medical treatment or advice? YES/NO
If yes, please give details

6 Any other comments

Signed by Employee .... Date...................

Signed by Line Manager.................................. Date...................

Appendix 2

Examples of underlying causes

Organisation related:

Management style
Poor internal communications
Restructuring/delayering
Culture of organisation to take 'sickie' days off
Harassment/victimisation in the workplace
Unattractive reward package
Sick building syndrome
Personality clashes with colleagues/boss.

Job related:

Boring/repetitive work
Lack of training/guidance
Over/under worked
Unreasonable deadlines/demands made
Work hazards
Unpleasant working conditions
Worn out/broken down equipment.

Personal issues:

Family care

Moonlighting in second jobs
Social commitments
Domestic/financial problems
Personal sickness/disability
Addictions to alcohol/drugs, etc
Practical problems with accommodation/transport
Emotional upsets, eg bereavement, divorce.